Blackbeard
the pirate

The exciting story
of the most famous pirate of all time.
A hero turned villain and later
into a legend.

© Blue Planet Productions S.L
28017 Madrid

© Blackbeard the Pirate.
ISBN: 978-84-608-4933-9

Ilustrations: Oscar F.
Cover and layout: Jesús Castillo.

For more information:
www.blueplanettales.com
info@ blueplanettales.com

There was a time
when the oceans were
the most dangerous
places on earth. And it
wasn't because of large
sea monsters or anything.
It was because pirates
had made the oceans into
their home.

A former sailor in the British Royal Navy was the one who stood out among all the pirates. He had sailed the Caribbean like a man ever since he was a little boy. Edward Teach was his name, but he was known as Blackbeard. When the Spanish War of Independence ended, he lost his job and joined up with a pirate ship and soon became captain.

Thus began the legend of the most famous pirate of all times.

He navigated at the helm of Queen Anne's Revenge along the East Coast of the US and the Caribbean islands. His mission was to rob merchant ships and sell their bounty in the cities. And he did so with great skill.

One summer morning he spotted a distant merchant ship that contained great bounty. They quietly snuck up on it.

When they were close, they raised their pirate flag and started the pursuit. The merchant ship fled towards a shallow cove that Blackbeard knew like the back of his hand. This was his best trick.

Little by little he closed in on them, firing cannons from time to time. At first it was to trap them. Later, he fired at the ship to make sure it couldn't sail any more. When the vessels were side by side, the horrible pirate turned to his men and shouted, "All Aboard!"

All of his pirates attacked the unarmed merchant sailors and the unfair battle began. Blackbeard, who was as tall and strong as a basketball player and had a large, dark,

bushy beard, soon joined them. Thanks to his trick that seemed like magic to the sailors, he became the most feared pirate on all the seas.

He placed slow-burning cannon fuses around his face so after they went out, his face and fiery eyes were enclosed in a cloud of smoke. This made him look like a demon from the underworld.

Faced with Blackbeard's loaded guns and powerful sword, the enemy surrendered and once again he took off with their treasures.

Soon he became one of the most feared pirates in the world. Some governments made an agreement with him: they wouldn't try to capture him if he didn't attack their ships. He also promised to give them a part of the bounty he won in each of his captures. But some governments didn't make any such agreement with him. One day while sailing along the coast, he ran into a Royal Navy ship.

They tried to sink him with their cannon fire. But Blackbeard responded with great violence. A cloud of cannon shots fell on the military ship and they fled for their lives. The pirate could have sent them to the bottom of the sea, but after some thought he said to his crew, "Let them go. They'll spread the word about what happened and everyone will know not to mess with Blackbeard." The pirates yelled insults to the fleeing cowards. From that day on his fame grew, and so did his problems.

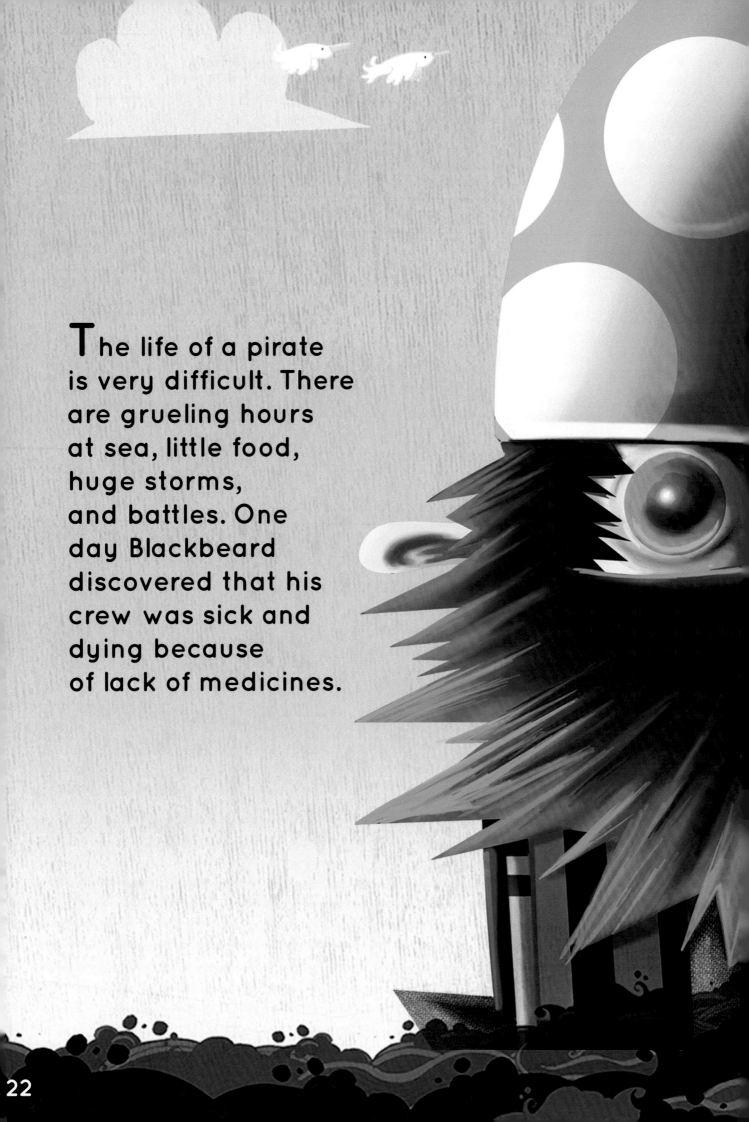

The life of a pirate is very difficult. There are grueling hours at sea, little food, huge storms, and battles. One day Blackbeard discovered that his crew was sick and dying because of lack of medicines.

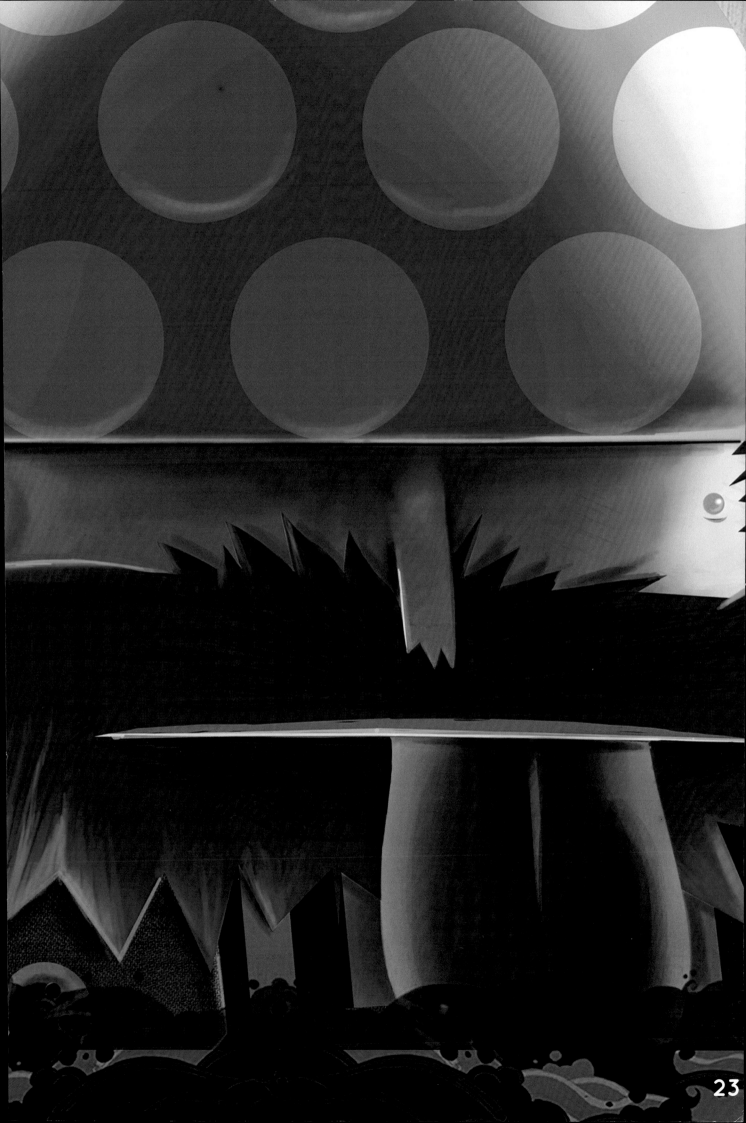

He couldn't buy them or steal them. So he gathered up his courage, collected all his ships and headed to the port in the city of Charleston.

He blocked the port and kidnapped some noblemen. They would be set free in exchange for medicines for his men. In order to save their people, the leaders had to agree to his deal. But they never forgave him, and this was the beginning of the end for the infamous pirate.

During the following months, they observed him up close, waiting for a moment when he wasn't paying attention. One fall morning in 1718, Blackbeard was on

his ship with only 19 men in poor condition since they had been drinking the night before, when he saw two Royal Marines vessels approaching.

Since he wasn't in any condition to fight he ducked into some neighboring channels trying to get away, but his ship ran aground and they had to fight man to man. He prepared his guns, sword, and the burning cannon fuses in his beard, and embarked on a suicidal battle against his enemies who had three times as many men.

Fighting like true pirates, they never gave up and they even succeeded in sinking one of the ships. But it wasn't enough. When they boarded the second, it became a battle to the death. Blackbeard's men fell one by one, until he and the Royal captain came face to face.

The demon of the seas fought savagely, but the captain had help from his men and finished off the pirate rather quickly. This was the end of Blackbeard, and the beginning of his legend.

Upon arrival in the city, Lieutenant Robert Maynard chose a barbaric way to display his victory in public so that pirates everywhere would know what would happen if they dared to challenge him. He cut off Blackbeard's head and placed it on the front of his ship as he was arriving at Virginia. As he pulled into the port everyone was shocked to see the pirate's head.

After he came off the ship with the head in his hand, showing it off all over town, he hung it in the Hampton courtyard.

That day, everyone in the city went to sleep knowing that one less pirate roamed the seas and one more hero was added to their legends.

1. What work did Blackbeard do before becoming a pirate?

A. He was a sailor in the Royal Navy
B. He sold fish at the port
C. He worked on ships that came back from the war

2. What seas did Blackbeard sail?

A.   The East Coast of America and the Caribbean
B.   The British coasts
C.   The Spanish coasts

3. What did Blackbeard do to appear more terrifying?

A.   He put burning cannon fuses in his beard
B.   He put on devil horns
C.   He carried three swords

4. What was the name of the ship he was in charge of?

A.   Queen Anne´s Revenge
B.   Queen Victoria
C.   Elizabeth the Second

5. What do pirates shout when they attack a ship?

A.   All aboard
B.   Let's get them
C.   To the sails and the battle

6. How did Blackbeard prevent some governments from pursuing him?

A. He gave them part of his bounty
B. He politely asked them not to
C. He hid out all day

7. What did Blackbeard need when he took over Charleston?

A. Medicine
B. Food
C. Rum

8. Who did he kidnap to get what he needed?

A. Some noblemen
B. Some beautiful girls
C. Some poor children

9. Why couldn't he fight at the beginning of his last battle?

A. Because there were few of them and they had been drinking
B. Because he didn't fight against Royal Army soldiers
C. Because he was a coward and always ran away

10. Where did they hang Blackbeard's head as a warning to other pirates?

A. On the bow or front of the ship, and later in a courtyard
B. On the ship's main sail, and later in the port
C. In the captain's cabin, and later in his living room at his home

1. What work did Blackbeard do before becoming a pirate?

A. He was a sailor in the Royal Navy

2. What seas did Blackbeard sail?

A. The East Coast of America and the Caribbean

3. What did Blackbeard do to appear more terrifying?

A. He put burning cannon fuses in his beard

4. What was the name of the ship he was in charge of?

A. Queen Anne´s Revenge

5. What do pirates shout when they attack a ship?

A. All aboard

6. How did Blackbeard prevent some governments from pursuing him?

A. He gave them part of his bounty

7. What did Blackbeard need when he took over Charleston?

A. Medicine

8. Who did he kidnap to get what he needed?

A. Some noblemen

9. Why couldn't he fight at the beginning of his last battle?

A. Because there were few of them and they had been drinking

10. Where did they hang Blackbeard's head as a warning to other pirates?

A. On the bow or front of the ship, and later in a courtyard